About The Authors

Richard W. Peters, M.D. is a pathologist and head of a laboratory in Michigan. He is an Advanced Master Gardener and has grown dahlias for 20 years. The last 12 years have seen him as a lecturer on dahlias and as a consummate exhibitor at many Midwest Dahlia Shows. Presently, he is Membership Co-Chairman of the American Dahlia Society, President of the Midwest Dahlia Conference, and President of the Grand Valley Dahlia Society.

Steve Nowotarski is a member of the Executive Committee and Chairman of Garden Dahlia Committee of the American Dahlia Society. An award-winning hybridizer of new dahlias, Steve also volunteers as Director of the Dahlia Display Garden at Planting Fields Arboretum in Oyster Bay, New York. A confirmed exhibitor of show dahlias he also is in the forefront of the garden dahlia and container dahlia movement. He has produced a DVD "Growing Dahlias in a Container" that explains in simple terms the method of growing successful dahlia container gardens.

Kevin Larkin co-owns Corralitos Gardens, a mail order nursery specializing in dahlias. He is President of the Monterey Bay Dahlia Society and the Pacific Southwest Dahlia Conference and Chairs the Research and Education Committee of the American Dahlia Society. He consults for Gowan Company and is on the Pest Management Committees of the California Association of Nurseries and Garden Centers and the Salinas Valley Grower/Shipper Association developing agricultural and horticultural pest management products.

Acknowledgements

Since this manual was designed for beginners, all chapters were read by Amy Recor, who raised her first dahlias last season. Then they were evaluated by Mac Boyer, Ron Miner, Richard & Betty Rejman, and Wayne Shantz who have been in the dahlia business for decades. A careful check for clarity was then done by Nancy Peters. Finally, a large number of hours was devoted by Steve Demos, M.D., who put the whole project together so that the printer could make some sense of it all. We are grateful for their input and assistance.

Raising Beautiful Dahlias
The Easy Way

edited by Richard W. Peters, M.D.

Presenting Major Insights

Into the Care and Feeding

of the Dahlia

The American Dahlia Society

Printed in The United States of America by
Custom Service Printers.

ISBN 0-9771292-2-5

Computer Graphics and Page Layout by
Steven S. Demos, M.D.

Table of Contents

Country Charm

Photo by Dan Franklin

Introduction
by Wayne Shantz

The American Dahlia Society takes great pride in offering a primer for those of you who enjoy the dahlia. The dahlia features some outstanding qualities that set it apart as special. Although many growers consider it a fall flower, in most regions it will begin blooming in early July and continue flowering throughout a growing season until frost.

With you in mind, the American Dahlia Society has focused on creating this easy to read manual that will offer you increased pleasure in your dahlia ventures. You will find simple "how to" approaches to the finer growing methods of dahlias and information on soil preparation, planting, maintaining the garden, storing procedures, and much more. All of this is provided by competent dahlia growers. If you follow the information in this manual, you will experience a new pride of ownership, and your garden will become a focal point for conversation. Indeed, your garden will be the talk of the neighborhood. It may even become a site home in your community's annual garden tour. But most importantly, the garden will provide your friends, family, and you with many hours of colorful enjoyment.

For some of you who have never grown dahlias, you may ask, "Why grow dahlias?" To the extent that we know, the dahlia consists of at least 50,000 named varieties originating from around the world. These hybrids come in a multitude of shapes, colors, and sizes that will give you many textures and blooms over a long span of time, which are a few of its unique contributions. For comparison and contrast, ***Bonne Esperance***, a petite mignon single, has eight petals surrounding a central open center, and the entire bloom's diameter measures less than two inches. Conversely, in stark contrast, ***Emory Paul***, a large informal decorative, will produce a bloom that can grow over sixteen inches in diameter. Of course, such a spectacle and divergence will cause many to question how such dahlias can be a part of the same family or even be real, but they represent and do belong to the dahlia connection.

If you coax a plant into blooming early, you can enjoy dahlia blooms for up to four months, a quality worthy of consideration since few flowers boast of such endurance. The dahlia blooms majestically in the fall when days shorten and climactic conditions cool, which will cause the dahlia to clothe your garden with vibrant, showy colors. Hopefully this manual will encourage gardeners to grow a dahlia plant or two. So, do set aside personal fears, do catch the excitement train, do plant that tuber, and above all else, do get started. If you will employ this manual's approach, I can heartily assure you that the dahlia in its opulence will not disappoint you for it truly creates its own splendor in space and time.

Amy Recor holding
Emory Paul

The American Dahlia Society is an organization with international membership set up to promote the dahlia. More than seventy member organizations are present in the United States and Canada. They function as Dahlia Clubs to show members how to raise these plants, put on demonstrations, and hold dahlia shows. We would encourage you to join your local dahlia club and also become a member of the American Dahlia Society. You can find additional information online: http://www.dahlia.org/

Chapter One

Where To Get
Dahlia Tubers

by Richard W. Peters, M.D.

Many commercial dahlia growers own and operate small businesses that were created because of their love and personal interest in the dahlia. They have spent many years growing these plants, and many are prominent members of the American Dahlia Society. A good number of them show their dahlias in regional

dahlia shows and have active programs to introduce brand new dahlia cultivars. The American Dahlia Society encourages you to seek out these growers by reading their advertisements in the *American Dahlia Society's Quarterly Bulletin*. The March issue devotes two timely articles that provide information about dahlias that have grown well across the United States and Canada. The article called the Fabulous Fifty lists and ranks all the varieties that have won at least 50 blue and higher awards in the shows for that year. The second article entitled Cream of the Crop lists the varieties that have received at least 15 combined blue and higher awards. These two articles summarize efficiently what varieties have performed well and will give you a good indication of the top show dahlias available. You can also click on the Colorado Dahlia Society's Web Page to see listings and pictures of these flowers: www.dahlias.net/supplierlst.htm, a commercial grower contact and www.dahlias.net/dahwebpg/Gallery/GalDirectory.htm that has much information.

Another reliable source of excellent cultivars is the local Dahlia Society. Almost all of them put on tuber sales in the spring. Look at this web site for the time, date, and location of the tubers sale of the society nearest to you: www.dahlias.net/adscontacts.htm The tubers are ones of which the growers have an excess, and they are offered for sale at reasonable prices. You also have the opportunity to visit with experienced growers and can "pick their brains" on how to grow these flowers. Who knows? They may even talk you into joining the Club!

A prominent retail store is another place to purchase dahlias. These dahlias may not possess the finest form of a show dahlia, but they almost always produce a good number of tubers and tend to grow well. Occasionally, these varieties lack the correct name, and on occasion do not reflect the type of dahlia that is in the package. However, these varieties are inexpensive, which is always worthy of consideration. If you do choose to start with this type of tuber, you should still grow dahlias with some success if you follow the wisdom provided in this small book. Our intention is to get you started properly; if successful, you will most likely migrate to the finer quality dahlias in due time.

You should also consider the size of the dahlias you are buying. Some plants are rather short, being only a foot or so in height (**Rembrandt; Bonne Esperance**) and others may rise to 7 feet (**Kenora Clyde; Kenora MACOP-B**). These are all beautiful dahlias, but you will need to be prepared to handle them beforehand. Most dahlias are 3-5 feet in height—growing somewhat taller in the Midwest and Eastern United States than in the Pacific Northwest.

Chapter Two

Site Selection
Soil Preparation and
Fertilizing

by Richard W. Peters, M.D.

Site Selection

The best site for growing healthy dahlias would be one that has at least 5 hours of sun per day. Some gardens will have areas of more shade to areas with full sun. As you study your dahlias, you will begin to know the varieties that are more shade tolerant and those that will only perform in full sun. If possible, also employ some protection from prevailing winds. Dahlia stalks are strong, but brittle, and wind can cause the laterals to break. In some cases, the entire plant will be flattened. Additionally, dahlias will not tolerate soils that have poor drainage. If there are puddles standing in your garden for any length of time, the dahlia roots may rot. Construction of raised beds is the easiest way to alleviate the poor drainage problem.

The site needs a readily available supply of water. You may successfully use overhead watering, but this practice has the disadvantage of the wasting water through evaporation and sprinkling areas that are not part of the garden. Overhead watering will also collect in the large blooms of the dahlia and can occasionally cause the stems to break from both the weight of the bloom and the added water. Most dahlia gardeners prefer soaker hoses, and this method avoids the negatives of the overhead systems.

Soil Preparation

A soil test is highly advised every 2-3 years, as it will outline the nutrient level of your garden. With the results of these tests in hand, you will be able to supply the fertilizer recommendations to bring the levels to the optimum needed for best growing results. November is an ideal month to do soil testing of the garden. The garden is now in its resting state, and the laboratories that perform soil testing are not busy. To do this, take a pint jar or plastic bag into the garden with your trowel. Select 3-4 sites and scrape away the top inch of soil. You will want to sample from the top of the scraped area down to about four inches. This is the area in which the dahlia tubers grow and the soil that you want to have tested. Dig a little hole and mix up the soil, taking a small handful to place in the container. Do this with the remaining sites. There will be about a half pound of soil in your container. Shake the container well to mix. If you have an area of your proposed garden that appears much less fertile, it would be best not to mix the soil from that area into your sample but keep a sample from that area separate. It is likely that the results may be quite different.

Kits can be purchased to do your own soil testing, but these are not recommended. Many states have an agriculture college that has a soil-testing laboratory. This agency should be a good place in which to have soil tested. Excellent private laboratories are also available in many areas. You will receive a form from the laboratory asking specific questions, such as the type of crop you are growing in your soil. Don't bother to look for "dahlias", since it will not be listed. If you check "potato" you will have chosen a plant that somewhat has the same needs as a dahlia. Make sure to write "dahlia garden" somewhere on the slip so that the analyst will see it. Understand that most laboratories charge a small fee for this service.

The local horticulture agent may then review the results, and a full report is sent to you that shows the excesses and deficiencies of your soil and recommendations for product additions or deletions. The dahlia grows well with a pH from 6.5 to 7.0, which is just slightly acidic. If the pH is well out of range, it will be important to add an amendment that will adjust it back into the proper area.

If you have clay (heavy) soil, you will need to evaluate the site carefully. Dahlias will not stand for a site that forms puddles. They must have good drainage, or the tubers will rot. Dig deeply into the clay or better yet, consider putting in a raised bed. Railroad ties, 2 x 10 treated boards, etc, can be used to hold the new soil. An additional advantage to a raised bed is that the soil will warm more quickly in the spring, and the plants will begin to grow at a much faster rate. If raised beds cannot be considered, then add 4 inches of composed organic matter to the top of the soil and dig it in well with a spade or rototiller. The organic matter will allow for better aeration for the roots of the plants and will help to promote drainage.

If you have mostly a sandy soil, you will have the problem of water draining through your soil at a rapid rate and not being available to the roots of the plants for very long. This means that you will have to water the garden often for it to flourish. The water holding capacity of a sandy soil can be greatly improved by adding compost and digging it in.

If you have a loam soil, you are very fortunate. It will hold water much better than the sandy soil and will not puddle up like the clay soil. Again, adding composted organic matter will further improve the soil. Remember that good soil preparation for a dahlia garden is key to success, and all types of soil will need the compost.

What should you use for compost? Often this question is answered by what is available locally in the area. Examples are far ranging, and include turkey droppings, horse manure, cow manure, chopped leaves, mushroom soil, or any other organic matter that

is allowed to decompose in a pile for about a year. During this year, the bacteria, crustaceans, and fungi will work to decompose the fresh material into compost. If you add raw organic material before it is fully decomposed, there might be problems with burning of the plants and fungal diseases. It is very important that the organic matter be composted. A nice time to add the compost is in the late fall, as it can further decompose over the winter and early spring.

By adding the compost, the soil will develop a good structure, with improved aeration, water conservation, and necessary minerals. The soil will develop a good texture, and nutrients in the compost will become available to your plants as the organic matter is further broken down. Continue to add the compost each year, as it will tend to disappear because of breakdown. Be careful in the use of composted horse manure, as weed seeds pass easily through the horse's digestive system, and you can end up with thousands of weeds in your dahlia garden. Many horses that are in commercial stables are fed pellets and do not eat weeds in the pasture or hay. Those horse manures make excellent compost for a dahlia patch. Be very careful that the compost you chose does not contain long-acting herbicides (weed-killer) or heavy metal contaminants.

Fertilizing

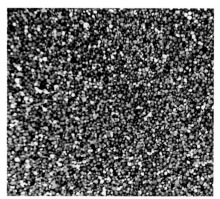

There are few areas in the growing of dahlias where there is a more striking difference of opinion among the growers than that of fertilizing. Some use dilute amounts of fertilizer in their drip systems, others apply fertilizer to the soil and to the leaves of the plants (foliar feeding), while some throw on 12-12-12, and others like bone and/or blood meal. A few use very little fertilizer at all. If you follow the directions of your soil test analysis, you have probably chosen the best way; you can then employ one or two dressings a season that are specific to what your garden lacks.

In evaluating the multitude of fertilizer types, knowledge of the three numbers listed on the bag is very helpful. The first number is the percent of nitrogen; the second is the percent of phosphorus, and the third is the percent of potassium. So a 100-pound bag of 12-6-10 would necessarily contain 12 pounds of nitrogen, 6 pounds of phosphorus, and 10 pounds of potassium.

Nitrogen (N) is an important part of the enzymes, proteins, and chlorophyll of plants, and plants lacking in this nutrient have yellowing of their leaves. Nitrogen will give lush green growth to plants, and with all of the chlorophyll available, the plant will make more food for itself. Nitrogen is not held very well by the soil and tends to pass through with each watering. Fertilizing with half the amount and then with the other half a month later is preferable to fertilizing with nitrogen all in one big dose. With the single, large application, the excess nitrogen filters into the groundwater and may end up in a nearby stream or lake. This causes undesirable algae buildup (green stuff in the lake).

Phosphorus (P) is necessary for strong root and flower development. Some gardens have been fertilized for years with 12-12-12, and the phosphorus levels have become extremely high with consequent problems in the growth of the plants and their proper tuber production. The reason for this is that phosphorus does not leach out of the soil readily—just the opposite of nitrogen. So by knowing that a high phosphorus level is present, you simply use fertilizers with low phosphorus. Over the next several years the phosphorus level will slowly drop.

Potassium (K) is necessary for overall vigor, stress resistance, and stem strength. It is often supplied as "potash". It tends to be held by the soil, but not quite as strongly as phosphorus. With good amounts of organic matter in a garden (supplied from the compost), potassium is most always adequate in amounts.

In gardens containing excesses of both phosphorus and potassium, the analyst may suggest urea as the best fertilizer to use. Urea is pure nitrogen without any phosphorus or potassium. This can be carefully added to the soil in the middle of June and then again in the middle of July. In early fall, nitrogen application is not recommended, which would create more leaf and stem growth. During this time the gardener would want the dahlia to intensify its bloom and tuber production.

Organic fertilizers of blood meal and bone meal are not very potent and are very slow to release their goodness to the plants. However, they do contain many of the 16 essential elements that are necessary for all plants to grow.

Chapter Three

Planting Your Dahlias

Richard W. Peters, M.D.

Starting Tubers Indoors

Many growers like to plant plants rather than tubers in the spring so that they will get much earlier blooms. Unlike tubers, the plants have a fully developed root system, so when they are planted, they start to grow immediately. Getting tubers to produce a fully developed root system will require starting the tubers indoors. To do this you will need a reasonably warm room or basement, fluorescent lights, and shelving to hold the plastic pots. In warmer climates, though, where frost is not a problem, you may plant your tubers in the ground earlier without the special nurturing, although some growers still start tubers inside for earlier blooms.

Don't think that a fluorescent light set-up is too involved and/or too expensive. The shop lights will be about $11 for each set up that holds two bulbs. You can get one cool white and one warm pink bulb for about $1.50 to $3 each. Get an inexpensive, adjustable metal shelving from the hardware store. You will want to have your fluorescent lights about an inch above your plants for them to do well, so you will want the shop lights to be suspended by a chain that can be adjusted for height.

If you only want to start a few dahlia plants, then you can use a sunny window. The plants can be moved outside during warm days and then brought in at night.

Deciding when to start putting the tubers into pots will depend on where in the country you reside. Perhaps the best indicator is when the people in your area plant their tomato plants outside. Subtract about 4-6 weeks, and that will give you the date to start your dahlia tubers indoors. In the upper Midwest, that time is about April 1st, which will then give a plant about 8 inches high that can be planted into the garden in the middle or end of May when there is no more fear of frost.

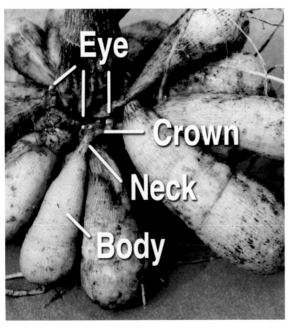

Anatomy of a Tuber

To start, a good understanding of a dahlia tuber is in order. The tuber looks similar to a small sweet potato, but can vary considerably from variety to variety. Generally there is an expanded, fleshy portion that is called the <u>body</u>. This then progresses forward to a thin portion called the <u>neck</u>. At the end of the neck is a bulging portion that is attached to the stalk of the mother plant. This is called the <u>crown</u>. A growth center from which a shoot will develop will always be found on the crown—never on the neck or on the body. The growth center in the crown is called an eye. As the eye grows into a linear stem-like structure, it is called a shoot. When the eye just begins to grow, the shoot may vary in color from a dark purple-red to a light green. Prior to this, the eye may appear as a small bump or even a depression in the crown. More than one eye may be present in the crown. If no eye is present, it is called a blind tuber and will not produce a plant.

Use a pot large enough to hold the tuber in such a manner that the crown is about ½ inch below the level of the soil in the pot and the eye is pointing upwards. Fill the pot with moist (but not wet) soil. Put a piece of waxed paper or aluminum foil over the pot so that the proper moisture remains. Place the pot in a warm area of your home (on top of the refrigerator, in the warm washroom, by the water heater, etc.). The plant can be in the dark and does not need sunlight to grow at this stage. Please remember one thing: use moist soil. The tendency is to water the tuber more and more because it is not producing a growing shoot. However, do not soak the tuber, as it will most likely rot.

Every few days, simply lift the cover off the pots and take a look at the surface of the soil. A small shoot will emerge when the tuber has awakened. At this time, the plant can be given a couple of tablespoons of water and will need to be put in light—either sun or fluorescent bulbs. When the young sprout is about 2-3 inches tall and forming leaves, more water can be given.

Two root systems will develop. One set comes off the body of the tuber and is called fibrous roots. They absorb water to feed the tuber and the plant. These roots will dry up and disappear in several weeks. The second set of roots begins to grow from the base of the plant, and they are called the tuberous roots. These will eventually grow into the primary roots that will support the plant, draw up nutrients, and produce the tubers for the coming season.

If multiple shoots come up, keep the single strongest and remove the others by clipping with a scissors or sharp knife.

Next, you will need to get your new, tender plants acclimated to the "cruel" outdoors. Young plants grown indoors can have their leaves scorched by the hot afternoon sun or their growth retarded by cold breezes. You might want to take them outside around 10 o'clock and give them a few hours of morning sun. Put them in the garage at night so that they become used to the cooler weather. After 3-5 days of this "hardening off", the plants can be put into your garden.

When to Plant

Whenever a new grower asks when the dahlias can be planted outside, we in the northern climates always seem to answer, "When the fear of frost is over" or "Anytime after Mother's Day". Actually some relevant data is available that may make the choice more scientific.

Every region in climates that have freezing weather will publish a "Frost Free Date". For instance: if a frost free date is May 15th, this indicates that throughout many years past, 50% of the time there was a frost after this date and the other half of the years, there was no frost after this date. One may wonder why they call it a "Frost Free Date" when in half the years there will be a frost. However a grower could find out this date from their local nurseryman, and this will give some information as to when to plant.

Another indicator used fairly successfully by experienced dahlia growers in the cold climates is to watch for the bloom of the lilac bushes. When they are in full bloom, you are ready to plant.

Climates in other areas of the country may not freeze at all. Planting in these areas is usually done when gardeners are putting out their tomato plants. Some growers are anxious to put their plants or tubers in the ground as soon as possible, thinking that they will get blooms in their garden more quickly than those who wait until the soil has warmed sufficiently. If one plants when the weather is cold and wet, dahlia tubers tend to rot in the ground in those conditions. Also, the cool to cold weather will not produce any growth, whether you are planting a dahlia plant or a tuber.

Planting early in cold areas of the country creates another problem. There is the ongoing risk of a late frost, causing the gardener to go out in the evening and cover up all the dahlia plants. Then the plants will need to be uncovered the next morning. There simply is no fun in this endeavor! It is best to wait until the ground has warmed and fear of frost has passed.

Planting Dahlia Plants in the Garden

If you are in an area prone to cutworms, you will need to take one of several possible precautions. If not, you will enter your garden the morning after you first planted only to find several of your plants chewed off at the base with the wilted plant lying dead on the ground. The cutworm is a green-grey worm about an inch long that comes out at night. It locates a tender stalk and wraps its body around the base of the stalk. Here it chews the stalk all the way through. It may then bury itself in the soil just beneath, and often the worm can be found buried down in the soil around the stump.

Cutworm damage can be controlled by taking a 1" by ½" slip of aluminum foil and encircling the stem of the dahlia with the foil. The plant is placed into the hole in the soil and covered over with remaining soil, and the foil adjusted to the correct level. This way, the cutworm will come out at night and detect the metal of the aluminum foil. It will move on to some other plant. The second method is a strange one, but it does work. Knowing that the cutworm likes to encircle the base of the stalk with its body and chew the tender stalk in two, you can place a finishing nail or a rounded type

Cutworm

of toothpick into the ground right next to the stalk. This inhibits the worm from encircling the plant's stem, and the cutworm will move on to another plant. Some growers feel they must douse their soil with insecticide to kill the worms. This probably is not very effective, as the worms are underneath the soil during the day.

Place a four or five foot stake next to the dahlia plant, and place a label on the stake. Again, remember that these are large plants, and planting about 2½ ft. apart will be just about right. Don't shade a short plant by surrounding it with tall varieties.

Planting Tubers Directly into the Garden

Many growers do not want to be bothered with the fuss of starting their tubers inside in pots, so they chose to plant the tubers directly into the ground. First dig a hole about 4 inches deep and place the tuber into the hole on its side. Try to make sure that the eye is facing upwards. Then use damp soil to fill up the hole. Put a stake in the ground next to the hole and attach the label tag to the pole. The tuber should not be watered at this time, as rotting may occur. Wait until the shoot appears, and then light watering can begin. Water fully when the leaves have come out on the plant.

Many growers like to put the stake in the ground right next to the dahlia tuber at the time of planting. By adding the stake later, one runs the risk of spearing the tuber. This may cause the tuber to rot, but it is rare. Other growers do not bother and will add stakes whenever the dahlia seems to need it.

It is not necessary to put fertilizer into the hole or on top of the soil at this time. Since nitrogen passes through the soil quickly, it would be a better practice to dress the soil with fertilizer after the leafage has been well established.

Chapter Four

Dangers to Avoid in the
Early Garden

by Richard W. Peters, M.D.

When shoots start coming up or when small plants are placed into the garden, a few items need consideration. We have already outlined the danger of the cutworms in chapter three.

Another problem to consider is the late spring frost. Watch the weather report for your local area very carefully. If there is a freeze predicted, you will need to cover your little plants. Folded newspaper, paper bags, or small squares of cloth can be used for this purpose. Remember that you will need to remove the coverings the next morning when the threat has passed.

Slugs and snails love to eat the tenderest areas of a dahlia plant, and of course this is the area that is giving the growth. The ends of laterals (side branches) and the tip of the plant are the areas that will be involved. There are multiple methods of controlling these land mollusks, such as surrounding each plant with a thin copper wire, small sharp rocks, or crushed egg- shells. Pots of dahlias can be protected by a rim of petrolium jelly put around the outside surface of the pot.

Slug

Snail

Shallow bowls filled half way with beer will attract slugs and snails to drink. They will be found the next morning in the bottom of the bowl—happy, but dead. Distributing old coffee ground around the plants will kill slugs, as they find caffeine to be toxic. Hand picking the slugs off plants in the garden can done, but only a few gardeners will participate in this endeavor!

There are two baits to use that are effective. Metaldehyde and iron phosphate products are available. The former can be detrimental to dogs and cats in the neighborhood, so care must be given in its use. The iron phosphate product is naturally found in soil, so it tends to dissolve and enter back into the soil in a benign fashion. Both are fairly effective.

Whatever method is chosen, be sure and deal with this problem early in the spring while the numbers of snails/slugs are small. A garden can be totally overrun by slugs at the end of the summer. They will devour most everything and will be present in massive numbers. Don't let this happen to either your dahlias or other garden plants.

Mule deer and white tailed deer will eat dahlias, as will rabbits and woodchucks (ground hogs). Moles do not eat dahlias, as they are carnivores, but pocket gophers and voles will dine extensively on the tubers. Controlling these mammals have made for some very interesting stories in the dahlia world.

Chapter Five

To Mulch or Not to Mulch

by Richard W. Peters, M.D.

*A dark colored mulch will draw increased heat
from the sun that can speed the growth
of the new dahlia*

For dahlia growers, the topic of mulching often finds them in opposing camps. One view accepts mulching as an extremely beneficial practice while the other looks on the activity with disdain. For you, experiment and decide which side of this question works the best.

Pro

A mulch of organic matter, such as chopped leaves, pine needles, grass clippings, crushed coconut shells, straw, among other mediums offer you a number of options for covering your garden with 2 to 4 inches of mulch. This covering will prevent weeds from growing among the plants and will preserve moisture by preventing rapid evaporation of water from the soil. A dark colored mulch will draw increased heat from the sun that can speed the growth of the new dahlia plants/tubers. You should not allow the mulch to touch the stalk of the dahlia. This precaution will prevent possible fungal diseases. In mid season if you remove some of the mulch you will see many roots of the dahlia plants on the interface between the mulch and the soil line. It seems reasonable that the roots must be using the fresh nutrients that the mulch offers. Mulch will also provide some protection of the dahlia clumps if an unexpected freeze comes before you dig the clumps in the fall. Obviously, in milder climates you would not have this concern, but you could deter tuber rot if you experience an excessive amount of rain. Finally if you choose to mulch you may provide a healthy environment through its humus and soil amending contributions.

Con

Mulch offers pests, such as slugs, snails, and earwigs, superb hiding places. Some growers prefer that their garden soil be totally free of mulch, weeds, and any structures that may serve as hiding places for these pests. If you choose to mulch, the possibility exists that you may have to resort to increased insecticide and snail bait usage in order to control these pests. The lack of mulch also allows you to observe accurately what is happening to the lower stalks of your dahlia plants. If you remove some of the lower leaves as the plants mature, you allow for better air circulation thereby combat powdery mildew problems. Unfortunately, mulch may increase the chances of mildew infestation.

The question has now come full circle, and you must decide what makes the most sense for you.

Chapter Six

Grooming the Dahlia Patch

by Richard W. Peters, M.D.

D ahlias start to grow when they find the right temperature, soil conditions, and water. In fact you might want to stay out of the way of some varieties, as their growth can be measured daily! Out-of-control growth can occur in these plants. Some people find this acceptable and don't mind the bushiness and the small blooms that result. You may wish to consider some or all of the following if you desire the larger, more perfect blooms that dahlias are noted for.

Staking and Tying

A large stake with the variety label tied on should be inserted next to the growing plant. Dahlia plants have strong stems, but they are brittle and will be broken by the wind. It is necessary in most instances to tie the laterals up properly. Proper tying also allows stems to grow straight and strong to hold the bloom in the proper position. Binder twine seems to be the most popular. The green binder twine is suggested rather than the usual tan, as it will blend in very nicely with the plant. Simply tie up the laterals of the growing plant and secure to the stake. You may wish to use a knot like you would tie up your shoe, because when you begin to cut the flowers, re-tying will often be necessary.

Tying can be a pain when you are in the garden and realize that a few plants need to be tied. You have to go back to the shed or garage to get the twine and come back out to the garden to finish

tying up the plant. An excellent plan is to put the ball of twine in a large soup can with a plastic lid. (The plastic lids can be found in the dog food section of the grocery store). Putting a small hole in the middle of the plastic lid will allow the strand of twine to come out of the can. Place several of these cans around the garden with an old knife or pair of aluminum scissors, so that they are handy when plants need tying up.

Some people really do not want to see a stake in their landscaped garden. If the plant is growing next to a fence, then use the green binder twine and tie it up to the fence. Another popular trick is to take a wire tomato cage or peony cage and turn it upside down. With a heavy pair of wire clippers, cut off the wires that normally would be put into the ground. Put the upside down cage carefully over the small plant, allowing the laterals to come out the edges of the cage. Now use the wires that were cut off of the cage to anchor the inverted cage. Do this by forming a "U" in the wire length with the wire cutters. The plant will soon grow up through the cage and hide its unsightliness. This will give some added support for the plant.

Topping the Plant

Pinch off the tip

When the plant gets around 4 sets of leaves coming out of its stalk, many growers like to pinch off the very tip of the plant. They feel that this allows the plant to produce equal laterals and form a more symmetric and bushy plant. If you chose to top your plants, simply find the top growing area and just push the plant tissue to the side. It will snap right off. In a few days small laterals will begin to emerge from the areas just above where the leaf meets the stem of the plant.

Other growers do not chose to top a plant. After about 4 sets of leaves, the plant will form a flower bud at its very tip. This bud will stop the plant since there is no further growth that can come from a flower bud. This way, the plant is stopped, and one gets to see a very early flower. Again, laterals will begin to emerge.

Disbudding

To get the most out of your dahlia plant's blooms and to improve the plant's total appearance, you might consider disbudding the plant. If this is not done, the side shoots will grow through the main blooms and the blooms will not look quite as nice as they could. This is really a quick and easy method, taking only a few moments every other day or so. Wait until morning or evening to

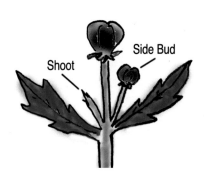

Remove two side growths (shoot and bud)

do the disbudding, as the plant has excellent turgor (stiffness) during these times. At the tip of every lateral (a side branch), there will be a terminal flower bud that is usually surrounded by two (or occasionally one) buds or shoots. Simply take your index finger and push the two side buds to the side until they break off. This will allow the central bud to become large and prominent. Its stem will develop to its fullest potential to hold the flower upright.

Disbranching

Disbranching means removing some of the laterals (side limbs) to concentrate all of the growing energy into the remaining blooms in order to maximize the size of those blooms. Now, much depends on the size of the bloom that the plant produces. If you have a plant, such as *Emory Paul*, you are expecting to see blooms with diameters greater than 12 inches in diameter. You will want to grow it in such a way that it will produce these huge blooms. In this case, about 3 laterals coming up would be best. So, you simply remove some of the smaller laterals by pushing them to the side until they break from the stem, or cut them with a garden tool. Trim off the lower leaves, especially ones that look ragged or half dead. This will keep your plant clean and healthy.

If you have a cultivar with smaller sized blooms, such as a ball form, you might want to have 6 or 8 laterals coming up to produce the blooms. So remove some of the extras so that you have the proper numbers. Another trick to control the growth of some dahlias is to pinch off the tiny shoots coming out at the base of the leaves below the flower that you just disbudded.

Watering

Dahlia plants are large and do require a moderate amount of water. In gardens composed mostly of sand, the hottest days in the summer will require watering every other day or maybe every day. Those gardens with heavy amounts of clay will need much less watering. One can get a feeling of the plants' need for water by observing them during the day. Some flagging (drooping) is almost unavoidable in the mid afternoon of a hot day, but excess flagging means a need for water.

A soaker hose system that puts water into the ground and not onto the plant is considered the most desirable watering method. However, many growers have little choice than to water overhead. If this is the method you use, water in the early morning hours so that the plants will have a chance to dry off during the day. With overhead sprinkling or rain, large blooms will hold a large amount of water leading to a broken stem. Some growers have been known to watch the weather reports and before a rainstorm they will take a small bamboo stake and tie up the stems of large flowers using twisty ties or pipe cleaners.

Chapter Seven

Growing Dahlias in a Container Garden

by Steve Nowotarski

W e are all aware of the tremendous number of garden containers available. The garden centers and even grocery stores are filled with them. Different sizes, shapes, colors and prices are available to the grower. In the gardening sections of all bookstores, large numbers of books are written on container gardening. These findings would lead one to believe that containers are the "IN" thing.

Gallery Rembrandt

Several reasons exist for this dramatic change. The increase in outside decks for summer living has created spaces that are in need of plants for decoration. Thus, many choose containers to fill in empty spaces around the home and the sides of pools. Many homes also lack the land space and can only accommodate smaller containers that might beautify a front walk or driveway. Containers may also augment roof and balcony gardens in apartment complexes, since most have limited space. Finally, many select containers because of their versatility; they can be moved from one area to another in a relatively easy manner, allowing for any desired changes in scenery.

After many years of careful selective hybridizing, dahlia growers have developed many beautiful, compact dahlias that lend themselves to container gardening. Growing dahlias in containers may be as simple as planting a single dahlia plant in an 8-10 inch pot. Or it may be as complex as incorporating a dahlia as the focal point in a 24-inch container with additional plant material to make the whole container a breathtaking garden statement.

Container gardening is simple, and there are no deep dark secrets to raising a successful container. But there are about six rules to insure both success and pleasure.

Here are the six simple steps:

1 Select a container.

2. Make a planting guide for placement of the plants in the container and select a dahlia plant and complimentary plants to go with the dahlia.

3. If the container is deep, place empty plastic water bottles or half-gallon plastic milk bottles in the bottom.

4. Find a good grade of potting mix and add to the container. In the top third mix in some slow release fertilizer and some water absorbent granules.

5. Arrange plants and fill in the spaces with the potting mix. Water in the plants and stand back to see the plants perform!

6. Periodically maintain the container garden including daily watering and fertilizing every two weeks.

The Six Steps In-Depth Process

1. Make the selecting of a container an enjoyable time. Aside from all of the wonderful containers in the garden stores, you can let your imagination run wild. You may find some intriguing and unique containers around the garage, attic, and storage shed that could include an old copper washtub from your aunt's garage, bean pots, wooden boxes, or old tin watering cans. How about an old wheelbarrow, wooden barrel, or (alas!) a chamber pot? Regardless, the container you select will need to have holes in the bottom for adequate drainage. A container chosen to give interest and one that is well planted will draw a lot of attention and compliments.

2. Selecting the proper dahlia and possibly additional plant material to go with the container is the next step. When using a small pot, select a low growing dahlia for a pleasing effect. Use an 8-10 inch pot and select **Gallery Art Deco** or **Gallery Rembrandt** to fill this type of pot. A perfect spot for either of these two dahlias will be found in your landscape or deck.

Gallery Art Deco

The finished product

With a large container of 20-24 inches or greater, you can create a mini-garden that will not only stand on its own but will act as a conversation piece and lend true character to your chosen location. The first thing to deal with is the color theme—for instance you select purple. All of the chosen plants selected will necessarily be compatible with purple, and **Gallery Art Nouveau** with its stunning cool purple will provide a useful focal point. The container will have the dahlia and two tall plants in the center that will feature structure, line and complementary foliage. In the picture, **Strobilanthes** "Persian Shield" and **Angelonia** "Angel face Blue" were selected as the tall plants to go with the dahlia. The outer portion of the container will have places for six plants, two each of three varieties. These varieties will add bulk to the pot by using **Coleus** "The Flume" and **Helichrysum** "Licorice Plant". The last two are trailing plants, **Calibrachoa** "Super Bells Blue". With the selection complete, planting can begin.

Placing empty water bottles in a container helps with weight issues.

3. Sufficient drainage holes are a necessity for every plant that is put into a container. With a large pot, place filler material in the bottom by using empty, capped, plastic water bottles. Fill the container about half full with the bottles. If you use this technique, the pot will be much lighter in weight and less expensive as well, since you will use less potting soil.

Note the bottles in picture.

4. The container is now ready for the soil mixture. Multiple recipes are available to the gardener, but a popular one uses 1/3 potting soil, 1/3 garden soil, and 1/3 of equal portions of vermiculite and composted cow manure. These items are mixed together thoroughly and added to the container. In the top 3-4 inches, add some slow-release fertilizer and water absorbent granules. The water absorbent granules are made of a potassium acrylamide polymer and can take in about 200 times their weight in water and will slowly release it to the roots of the plants. The material is non-toxic and breaks down into substances that plants can use. This one component can save a pot full of plants that an owner has inadvertently forgotten to water!

5. To plant, start in the middle with the dahlia and two tall plants. Remove the plants from their plastic containers and loosen the roots manually so that the plant's root system will be ready to spread out in its new home. Space them equidistant from one another, and firm the potting soil around the roots of the plants. The outer portion of the container will hold the other six plants, spacing the like ones opposite one another. Fill in any depressed areas with extra potting soil and water the container generously. This will help the new plants recover from transplant shock. Step back and admire your new creation.

6. A little maintenance goes a long way in keeping the container garden beautiful all season. Watering is by far the most important.

In the summertime, watering is almost an every day event, and when the days are very hot, twice a day watering may be necessary. A liquid fertilizer application every two weeks will be helpful for all of the plants, knowing that with all of the watering, nutrients will be flushed from the soil mixture.

Deadheading will ensure that more blooms will be produced during the season. If the spent blooms are not removed, the plant will go into a "seed production mode" and will intensify its efforts on making seeds and will tend to shut off the production of additional blooms. Every two weeks or so, some trimming of the plants is in order to present a neat appearance and to allow for airflow through the plant material.

Although container gardens seem to be much less susceptible to pests, you need to take a few precautions. Slugs and snails can travel up the sides of the container where they will devour the succulent growing tips of the plants. The treatment of these is nicely outlined in chapter four. Flying pests, such as aphids can be removed with a strong spray of cold water from a hose. Spider mites will cause the leaves to turn brown, starting at the bottom of the dahlia plant. A strong spray of cold water to the undersurface of the leaves will wash them off the plant, and they usually die where they land. If you continue to experience difficulties, spray the underside of the leaves with insecticidal soap, which will usually rectify this problem.

You can now place your completed dahlia garden container in the chosen location, comfortable in the knowledge that you can easily move it to other locations to suit individual needs. For additional help, a few Web Pages are available for your perusal: www.containerdahlias.com is a picture review of additional container plans using dahlias. www.verwer-dahlias.nl/ is loaded with pictures of dozens of low growing dahlias, including the Gallery, Melody, and Happy Single series. An array of container designs with named plants is listed at www.provenwinners.com, and only a central dahlia is needed.

Chapter Eight

The Use of Dahlias as Part of the Total Garden

by Steve Nowotarski

Ed Haugan's Garden

D ahlias are a wonderful addition to a garden. While many growers dedicated to exhibition tend to have all of their dahlia plants in an "orchard of dahlias", many gardeners exist who would like to use dahlias in the total garden environment. Dahlias can fit right in, and with a little planning, your garden will reward you with a long season of breath-taking panoramic displays.

The Dahlia Offers Many Favorable Attributes

1.   Color is the foremost quality in choosing a dahlia for the garden. Dahlias possess extremely colorful blooms with the exception of blue. You should not be surprised if guests visiting your garden quickly single them out and gravitate toward them.

2.   Form diversity in dahlias is extreme, going from a pompon dahlia, measuring an inch and a half in diameter to a huge dahlia of 14 inches. There are dahlias that are almost perfectly round, like a ball, and those that are spider-like and look like a chrysanthemum. Others are very formal while some are very irregular and look like they have had "a bad hair day".

3.   Bloom sequence is an important consideration in choosing plants for the flower garden. A plant that blooms continuously is preferable to those varieties that bloom in flushes and then wait many days to flush again. The smaller flowering dahlias, 6 inches or less, will generally provide more blooms for a season, exhibiting a colorful and lasting explosion.

4.   Foliage is very important in consideration of texture in the garden. Attractive and strong foliage can add much to the garden expression.

5.   The position of the dahlia in the garden can have an empowering effect. The dahlia should provide a distinctive quality to the garden but should not over-power other plants or be hidden in the shade of another. Therefore, selection of a dahlia variety for height becomes a major key to a visually appealing and balanced presentation.

6.   The dahlia may be used a little differently if you devote the garden solely to perennials or one consisting only of annuals. Such specific objectives have more to do with the planting techniques, which we will discuss later.

Take a closer look at these considerations now and how they can enhance our garden

Color

Ed is taking over his neighbor's garden, too!

If the dahlia will be in a mixed garden, how will the color of the chosen dahlia get along with the colors of the existing plants? A basic understanding of the color wheel will help us with this. The dahlia color must be "happy" with what already exists. With such a palette of colors available in dahlias, this should not be a problem. Don't be afraid to let the dahlia make a bold color statement in the garden. If the other colors allow it, a yellow and red variegated dahlia such as *Gloriosa* will quickly become the focal point of your garden. Visitors will be entranced with this bright beauty. Do allow your imagination to run wild with the wide variety of colors that the dahlia offers.

Form

The great variety of dahlia forms needs to be considered so that the chosen varieties will best complement other plants and shrubs. You may want to avoid the huge, "dinner plate" dahlias, as it is fairly difficult to obtain the advertised size, and you will have only a few large blooms during the season. The largest cultivar, **Emory Paul**, will sometimes give only one bloom right at the end of the season. Stick to the 4-6 inch sized flowers. You will be rewarded with many blooms and plants that are easy to maintain. Plant height is a consideration. Many of the new low growing varieties require little to no staking. If you desire to stake taller plants, refer to Chapter 6. Today there are many new dahlia varieties available that will excite the gardener with their open-centered forms. These types are fast becoming popular, and the demand has caused some hybridizers to focus their efforts in this direction. Just this year growers have introduced the HAPPY SINGLE series from our friends in the Netherlands; the RIO series from California; and striking dark foliaged brown centered singles from New Zealand.

Bloom Cycle

The gardener should select those cultivars that are known to produce blooms all season long. Not all dahlias have this attribute. Some bloom in flushes, and there can be a wait of several weeks before the next flush of blooms appears. Several ways exist to ensure that you plant the more floriferous dahlias. For quick information, approach other local dahlia growers that may have grown a certain variety. Members of local dahlia societies can also lend considerable knowledge to your pursuit. Most dahlia growers are friendly and ready to help in any way that they can. You can also contact experienced growers on any of the several dahlia forums on the Internet. Commercial dahlia growers usually provide growing information in their catalogues, and Internet sites offer information as well. You will find that e-mail and telephone calls to growers will almost always be fruitful in finding proper selections for your garden. Several particularly floriferous varieties are listed at the end of this chapter.

Foliage

While foliage is important in exhibition dahlias, it's a whole other issue with the garden type of dahlia. Interesting and colorful foliage will add a great deal to the attractiveness of dahlias and the whole garden. Over the past few years there has been a proliferation of dark foliage dahlias. Some varieties have foliage so dark that they are almost black. Fortunately, many of these new dark foliage dahlias are now readily available to the general public. In the last few years, we have seen dahlias with foliage that could pass for ferns become available. These differing foliages can lend an interesting texture to the garden.

Position of the Dahlia in the Garden

It is important to place the dahlias so that they add to the whole garden picture. If tall varieties are chosen, they will need to be placed toward the rear, while low growing border types need to be placed in the foreground. Be aware of the color combinations with the surrounding plants. A common mistake exists when you plant a dahlia tuber in the back of the garden with a clump of daisies immediately in front. If you know that your selected variety will be tall, you will plant it near the back; the daisies, although not as tall, will come up quickly and severely shade the dahlia. Consequently, the dahlia does not grow because of the shade, and you become discouraged. One trick is to grow the dahlia in a gallon-sized pot until it gets about 18" tall after which you can transplant it near the daisies and sufficient sunlight is now provided. Another trick is to plant the dahlia in a terraced garden where you can place it in the upper steps and still have it free of being shaded by other plants.

Ed Haugan's side garden

Type of Garden Where Dahlias Are Planted

Ed's garden

Including dahlias in a fully established perennial garden presents some challenges. Generally perennial gardens become rather dense after several years. By including dahlias, the root systems of the existing plants may be disturbed. Look for an area where a dahlia may be buried into the ground with a dahlia already established in a 2-gallon plastic pot. A you can place a variety like ***Magic Moment*** in a pot and nurture it to develop a good root system. Then you place the entire pot with the growing dahlia deep into the ground, making sure that the top edge of the pot measures about an inch below the level of the soil line. A further advantage is that the pot will help prevent perennial roots from encasing the dahlia tubers. This encasement is one reason why a dahlia may not perform well during its growing period. At the end of the season, the pot can be easily dug out of the garden without damaging the dahlia clump or the roots of the surrounding plants. An additional plus is that the dahlia can be stored successfully in the pot over the winter.

Planting dahlias in an annual garden is quite easy if the garden is planned with knowledge of the growth characteristics of the annuals. Since the annual garden is generally more colorful than a perennial garden, dahlias can be chosen with powerful colors including blends and even the beautiful bi-colored and variegated types. In a mixed annual border alternating a low growing dahlia with contrasting foliage annuals can make a very dramatic statement. For example, the dark foliages of low growing dahlias like the HAPPY FACES series alternated with any of the gray foliage annuals will frame the garden in a delightful way.

It is important to remember that the dahlia is, in most cases, a sun-requiring, robust plant. Its peak blooming period is late summer and early fall. This late blooming cycle will be very useful in an annual garden where by late August most annuals are showing the stress of the hot summer and their blooming cycle is about over. It is just at this time that the much admired dahlia steps forward to carry the garden. With the addition of colorful dahlias in the garden, you can be sure of a longer flower season.

Visitor admiring Ed's garden

Recommended Varieties of
Floriferous Cultivars

Magic Moment
Long Island Lil
Arabian Knight
Karma Pink Corona
Kenora Jubilee
Gloriosa
Honka
Melody Allegro
Ryecroft Jan

Back View of Spartacus

Photo by Steven S. Demos, M.D.

Chapter Nine

Dahlia Pest Management

by Kevin Larkin

K eeping your dahlias healthy and pest free does not have to be difficult if you follow a few steps that can result in a very efficient pest control program. The first step is to select healthy stock. Vigorous, actively growing plants are your best defense against insects and diseases. Start with healthy roots or plants, plant them into healthy soil and provide them with proper nutrients, light, and water. The second step is to observe your dahlias on a regular basis to see how they are doing and what is going on in the various parts of the plants. Monitoring your dahlias through the season is the most important activity you can perform to prevent or head off problems early. The third step is to properly identify pest and disease problems and determine if they are actually causing damage to your dahlias. You don't need to attack every bug you see in the garden. In fact a strategy like that will backfire and result in worse problems in the long run. The final step is to implement the correct control measures at the correct time and only as needed. Your garden's ecosystem includes a variety of organisms that as a whole can be managed so that you have an even balance between the beneficial and pest components. Excessive or improper treatment can wipe out the beneficial insects and cause additional pest problems that would be naturally controlled in a balanced system. These steps combined constitute an integrated pest management program that will help keep your dahlias healthy and productive.

Cultural Control

Everything you do in preparing for and growing your dahlias can impact the pest populations that you may later face. The simplest and often most effective pest management solutions are those that involve altering a cultural practice to prevent or reduce a pest or disease problem. Several ordinary gardening practices are illustrated below indicating ways they may be used to minimize pest problems.

Sanitation

Keep your garden free of refuse piles, stake piles, and diseased or dead plants. These can act as breeding grounds or can attract insect pests and can be the source of disease infestations. Keep weeds to a minimum to decrease competition with the dahlias' root systems.

Tillage

Till your soil when it is dry to minimize compaction and encourage good aeration to promote soil dwelling beneficial microorganisms. In climates that have freezing temperatures during the winter, tilling the soil in the fall will bring up eggs and larvae of pests that will be destroyed by the freezing of the ground.

Compost

Apply good quality compost to reduce root diseases, enhance nutrient uptake, and properly hold and distribute water. There are several excellent books that explain how to make your own compost pile, and the agriculture extension services in each state will also have some very good literature. You can also learn about composting from someone with experience. You want to make sure it is completely finished cooking (no heat is being generated in the compost pile) and that it contains no deleterious components, such as poisons, long-acting weed killers, and heavy metals.

Planting timing

Plant dahlia tubers only after your soil has warmed to at least 55 degrees. Planting into cold soils can result in rotting of tubers. Dahlia plants are less prone to this and can be planted earlier in the season into cooler soils.

Plant spacing

Greater distance between plants promotes light penetration and air movement that reduces leaf diseases.

Irrigation method

Overhead irrigation from lawn sprinklers promotes leaf and bloom diseases. If you must use overhead irrigation, time the watering for very early in the morning to allow the plants to dry out as early in the day as possible. Irrigation also impacts weed growth. Drip irrigation concentrates the water where you want it, helping keep open areas free of unwanted weeds.

Nutrition

Well-nourished dahlias are the best defense against pests and diseases. Excess nitrogen promotes lush growth, which may in turn create situations that create leaf diseases.

Staking

Adequately staked plants that are growing tall and with leaves off of the ground are less prone to leaf diseases and will also act as a deterrent for soil dwelling pests like earwigs, slugs, and snails.

The use of mulches

Mulches reduce weed growth and can also moderate soil temperature. But, mulches can also harbor pests like slugs, earwigs, and even mice. Refer to Chapter 5.

Biological Control

Biological controls occur in your garden even if you don't realize it. There are many beneficial organisms above ground and in the soil that routinely keep pests in check. If you can recognize them and encourage them to do what they do naturally, your garden will thrive.

Lady bug

The most visible biological control is the action of beneficial insects attacking pest insects by direct feeding. Examples include ladybugs, lace wings, praying mantis, syrphid flies, and numerous tiny wasps. You can increase their presence by purchasing the insects, such as ladybugs, and releasing them into your garden. Care must be taken if using insecticides to minimize the destruction of the beneficial insects.

Minimize the use of broad-spectrum products such as organophosphates, oils, and pyrethrum. Spray only in the evening or early morning when beneficial insects are less active. Beneficial insects vary by region, as does their preferred habitat, so it is best to inquire locally from a horticultural specialist what works best in your area.

Lacewing

Less visible is the action of beneficial organisms in your soil. A healthy soil is well aerated with good structure, and these features encourage soil organisms (mostly fungi and bacteria) that work to keep soil disease to a minimum. High quality composts contain microorganisms that promote nutrient uptake and reduce soil diseases. There are also beneficial soil insects that attack soil dwelling pests like wireworms and centipedes.

Centipede

Other types of biological control involve the application of naturally occurring compounds that exhibit controlling traits. *Bacillis thuringiensis* and *Bacillus popilliae* are naturally occurring soil bacteria used to control larvae and beetles. Plant extracts from the neem tree (*Azadiracta indica*) are used to control insects and diseases. Neem oils are effective at controlling foliar diseases like powdery mildew. The non-oil based neem extracts are effective insect growth regulators that can help control whiteflies, leafhoppers, and other foliar pests. Another plant extract, pyrethrum, from the chrysanthemum (*Chrysanthemum cinerariaefolium*) paralyzes many insects and has a very broad range of activity. There are also several beneficial parasitic nematodes that can be applied to control larvae and soil dwelling pests.

Specific Control Recommendations

These recommendations are based on pest control strategies that use naturally occurring compounds refined to be used in the garden for specific uses. It is important to follow the application instructions supplied with these products and to use them only when it is necessary. Most of these products are very safe to handle, but it is important that you follow all of the safety precautions recommended by the manufacturer on the product labels.

Slugs and Snails: Refer to Chapter 4.

Earwigs

Earwigs are nocturnal feeders and can do tremendous damage in a very short period. They nest under stepping stones, landscape timbers, leaf piles, and just about anywhere else that is dark and moist. Trapping is an

Earwig

effective control strategy for these pests. You can attract them to 5" pieces of bamboo, plastic pipe, wet rolls of newsprint, or liquid filled traps set near where you observe damage. Check your traps daily and empty them into a container of soapy water in order to kill the earwigs.

Cutworms: Refer to Chapter 3.

Larvae and Beetles

Striped cucumber beetle

Larvae and beetles will chew on leaves, buds, and blooms. In small numbers they may not need controlling, but they often can cause significant damage and you will have to implement some type of control strategy. The most damaging of these include Japanese Beetles, European Corn Borers, and Cucumber Beetles. There are several effective biological insecticides that can be used to control these pests. The strategies that are mentioned will work on most other larvae and beetles that may infest your dahlias.

Japanese Beetles live most of their lives as grubs in the soil under lawns feeding on the roots of the grass. Targeting this life stage to control is the most efficient and least disruptive to other beneficial insects. Products containing "Milky Spore" bacterium (*Bacillus popilliae*) spread on the lawn will kill the developing grubs. This significantly reduces the number of adult beetles and has a lasting effect if done properly. The adults can travel from yard to yard, so if you can get your neighbors to follow the same practice you can effectively clean up the whole neighborhood.

Japanese Beetle

European Corn Borer and Stalk Borer are worms that feed on leaves, stems, and buds of dahlias. The borers will bore into the stalks and may cause them to collapse. Their primary host is corn, so if you are in a corn-growing region you may experience heavy pressure. Products containing the soil bacterium *Bacillus thuringiensis (Bt)* can be sprayed or dusted on the foliage at the first sign of damage. Bt products will break down in a few days in direct sunlight so you may have to repeat this treatment. This may have to be done several times during the season in areas of heavy pressure.

Striped and Spotted Cucumber Beetles are lime green and have either black spots or stripes on their shells. They are very mobile and feed on open dahlia blooms. They migrate into dahlias on hot days and may build to very large numbers in a very short period of time. Sprays or dust containing the plant extract pyrethrum will knock down the adult cucumber beetle. You should target treatment to the blooms only and treat in the evening or very early morning when beneficial insects are less active. Pyrethrum, while natural and safe to people and pets, is indiscriminant in its activity on beneficial insects. This treatment will only affect those adult beetles that are sprayed, so repeat treatment may be needed under severe conditions. These insects are

Spotted cucumber beetle

strongly attracted to yellow which has prompted the use of traps made by smearing yellow cards with sticky materials and hanging them around the garden to trap the adults that land on them. These traps in conjunction with pyrethrum spray and hand picking can limit damage significantly.

Aphids and Leafhoppers

Aphids and Leafhoppers cause twisting and stunting of new growth and may contaminate opened blooms and shed "honey dew" on the plants they infest and thereby attract ants. They also carry several dahlia viruses. You should have a low tolerance for their presence since they could affect your entire garden.

Aphids

Aphids appear in colonies on shoot tips and unopened flower buds. Isolated colonies should be removed by breaking off the infested shoot or leaves. This practice will reduce spreading. You can control heavy infestations with insecticidal soaps, horticultural oils or neem-based products. The oils are very effective but can harm beneficial insects and may spot blooms and foliage so avoid spraying during hot spells and spray in the evening or very early morning when beneficial insects are less active.

Leafhoppers are more mobile and can be more difficult to control. They can increase in numbers very quickly so it is wise to monitor closely when you first detect them. You may need to act very quickly following the first sign of their presence to prevent severe damage. They can be controlled by spraying with horticultural oils, pyrethrum, or neem extract.

Additional Diseases Affecting Dahlias

Dahlia Smut

Dahlia smut appears as small white spots, usually on the lower leaves. It occurs in areas of high summer rainfall or where overhead irrigation is used. Avoid over-head irrigation if possible. In areas of high rainfall the disease is very hard to prevent. If you remove smut-infected leaves as soon as symptoms appear, you can reduce spread to uninfected leaves. Spraying agricultural lime on the soil at the base of the plants early in the season may also reduce the infection level.

Dahlia smut

Botrytis

Botrytis first appears as gray or white mold on dahlia blooms. You minimize botrytis by regularly removing spent blooms and clearing away all dropped petals and leaves in the plant canopy. Avoid overhead irrigation if possible or irrigate early in the morning so that your plants will dry out as early in the day as possible. During extremely rainy conditions it may be virtually impossible to control botrytis without stripping all the flowers from your dahlias.

Botrytis

Powdery Mildew

Powdery mildew appears as white powder (spores) on the tops of leaves on the lower part of the plant. The appearance of spores indicates the infection occurred 2-3 weeks earlier and will now spread by the movement of the new spores. Spraying or dusting new growth with sulfur containing fungicides is very effective at preventing new infection. This should be repeated every 3-4 weeks to keep the infection level to a mini-

Powdery mildew

mum. Spraying with potassium bicarbonate containing fungicides will destroy the white spores. This should be repeated every 10-14 days to reduce new infection. In areas chronically prone to powdery mildew, plant dahlias at a spacing that will allow plenty of air movement to reduce the relative humidity on the leaf surface.

Viruses

Viruses are not unusual in dahlias. Dahlia Mosaic Virus (DMV) is the most common, but there are at least 10 other viruses that can affect dahlias. Symptoms range from leaf discoloration, leaf and shoot twisting, and overall stunting of the plant. It is nearly impossible to identify which virus is present without specific testing. Your dahlias could come to you already infected or may become infected in your garden. Virus expression varies between varieties and can vary depending on the level of infection and other growing conditions of your dahlia. Leaf discoloration, stunting, and shoot twisting that cannot be attributed to leafhoppers, aphids, or some other insect is probably a sign of virus. Affected plants should be removed and disposed of to prevent spread to other healthy plants.

Conclusion

Growing dahlias properly can offer many advantages for you, especially if you maximize your productivity with preventive strategies to reduce damage from unwanted problems. Applying integrated pest management while following the other guidelines in this manual will dramatically reduce your pest problems and provide your plants with the best possible growing conditions. The most effective pest management strategies are those that prevent pest damage and reduce the need to implement control measures. In short, try to do everything you can to avoid having to spray in the first place, but if you chose to spray, make sure to read the label, following it precisely in order to select the right and least toxic product.

Vase of Dahlias

Photo by Nancy Peters

Chapter Ten

Cutting Your Blooms

by Richard W. Peters, M.D.

Elsie Huston

Photo by Steven S. Demos, M.D.

B looms should be cut early in the morning when the plant still has plenty of turgor (plant cells full of fluid; the opposite of wilted). Take a knife or sharp scissors and cut the stem at an angle to the desired length. Pull off the leaves that will be under water in the vase you will be using. Leaves under water will increase the production of bacteria, algae, and fungi that, in turn, cause the pores in the stems to become clogged. When the pores are clogged, the flower will not last very long. Put the flowers immediately into containers of cool water and bring into the house to be arranged.

Use of a flower preservative in the water is very highly recommended. If you use only water, in a couple of days, the vase's water will be a cloudy green, and the flower will only last 4-5 days. Several more days can be added to the flower's life if you use the preservative. You can purchase cut flower preservative from a garden store, nursery, florist, or any store selling cut flowers. You should expect to pay no more than 10 cents to make up a quart of preservative.

The flower preservative contains three elements that are crucial to prolonging the life of your cut blooms. In order for the preservative to work properly, it is VITALLY IMPORTANT that the directions be followed in order to give the proper concentrations of the three elements. If there is too much water, the concentration of the three elements will be too dilute to work properly.

These elements are:

1. A biocide is present which will kill the bacteria, fungus, and algae.

2. A sugar is included to keep the cells of the flower, stems, and leaves alive. When the plant's cells die, then the bloom dies.

3. A buffer is present to lower the pH of the water. Flowers will take up water more easily if the water is somewhat acidic.

Aside from using a flower preservative, you can extend the life of a bloom if you keep it in a cool place away from the direct sun. The same is true of your dahlia plant outside in the garden. Many cool days will give blooms that seem to last forever, while in hot spells, the flower matures and dies much more quickly.

The final thing that you can do to extend the life of your dahlia blooms is to keep them away from sources of ethylene. This is a gas that is released by many fruits that are maturing. Apples, pears, tomatoes, etc. put out small amounts of ethylene gas which will cause the dahlia blooms to mature and die faster than they would had they not been exposed. Surprisingly, even very tiny amounts of ethylene can cause a marked change in the flowers.

Another Vase of Dahlias

Photo by Steven S. Demos, M.D.

You may have heard that blooms will last longer if you plunge the cut end under water and re-cut a small portion of the end of the stem. Recent research has shown that this is not the case. Therefore, it is unnecessary.

If you notice green, cloudy water forming in your vase after 3-4 days in spite of having used flower preservative, it may be that a large dose

dose of organisms have landed on your flowers out in the garden. You might then try using 1 part ordinary bleach in 10 parts of water. Plunge the cut stems into this solution for 30 seconds to kill the heavy number of organisms that are present on the stem. Then treat the blooms as stated previously.

Cut dahlias should last about 8-10 days or more. They will vary by the way they have been treated as well as how early in the bloom cycle you picked them. Do remember one thing: dahlias are not like roses. If you pick a dahlia bud, it will not open up into a full sized dahlia bloom. Picking a bloom at, or just before, maturity is best.

Much of this above information has been gleaned from Professors Terril Nell at the University of Florida and Michael Reid from the University of California Davis. They have, and still are doing, extensive research on how best to keep cut flowers in their prime for many days.

The large dahlia blooms are somewhat of a problem to display in the usual vase. You can find striking glass or crystal bowls that are large enough to hold these blooms. By cutting the stem off to just the right length, you can float the bloom in these bowls. There are also small glass donuts that can be purchased at garden centers that will allow the stem to go through the device and into the water, while the bloom rests on the glass donut. Another trick is to use a plastic pint container that you get when you buy cottage cheese, tub butter, or sour cream. Wash out the container and fill it half with water containing flower preservative. Drape the large bloom over the container, with its stem submersed into the water. The bloom usually has petals that will drape down, thus hiding the markings on the plastic tub. These floating dahlias are nice for the dinner table, as they are low and do not obstruct the views of your guests and family members.

The pompon dahlias are particularly well suited for petite flower arrangements in small bud vases. Even a single bloom in a tiny vase beside the dinner plates of your guests is a nice touch. Pompon dahlia blooms have a slightly longer lasting period than most dahlias.

Occasionally, you will find a bloom that totally wilts within a few hours of having been picked. It will look like it needs to be pulled from the vase and thrown away. You may want to try a technique that will often revive the wilted flower: Fill a vase with the hottest tap water; this is usually about 180 degrees or so. Recut the stem of the flower and plunge the cut stem of the flower into the hot water and just wait a few hours. Most of the time, the dahlia bloom will be totally restored. Then put the bloom back in flower preservative.

Floral foam is a popular item to hold dahlia blooms and plant material in their containers. Floral preservative is again recommended. Find a container that will hold the bricks of floral foam (maybe a bucket or small tub), and set the foam brick on top of the water. Leave it alone until it has submerged and filled with water. DO NOT DUNK the brick. Dunking will cause water to enter the brick from all surfaces and will prevent the air in the middle of the brick from escaping. Air pockets form in the middle of the brick, and when the end of flower's stem is resting in an air pocket, you will lose the bloom in a few hours.

Minerva Sunrise

Photo by Steven S. Demos, M.D.

Chapter Eleven

Digging, Dividing, and Storing Dahlias

by Richard W. Peters, M.D.

R ecovery of a clump of dahlia tubers at the end of the season can reward a grower by having many more plants for the garden. Remember that dividing a clump and planting the tubers will always give the same variety with the same color and size of the bloom. This is called vegetative (or non-sexual) reproduction. For example, by planting a tuber of *Zorro,* one will always get a large red bloom. On the flip side, sexual reproduction occurs when a dahlia seed is planted. The offsprings from the seeds will give a totally different flower. Remember that the dahlia seed gets half of its characteristics from the pollen parent and the other half from the parent that produces the seed. The resulting plants from the seeds of dahlias are almost always very different from the parents.

Remember that a dahlia grower does not have to dig up the clumps. A prominent grower came down with rheumatoid arthritis, and she could no longer do the heavy work of digging up the clumps at the end of the season. She was about to give up on dahlia raising, when she realized that all she had to do was simply purchase tubers every spring from a variety of sources. She also reasoned that she spent $100 every spring on marigolds, impatiens and petunias, so why not spend some on new dahlia tubers? Her new plan has allowed her to enjoy her dahlias without irritating her disease.

The final comment is that there are as many different ways of digging, dividing, and storing dahlia tubers as there are dahlia growers. Find one that works for you and stick with it!

Digging up Dahlia Clumps

If you live in an area that freezes in the fall, then you might want to wait until the killing frost comes. This is easy to recognize, as the dahlia plants turn black, and the leaves collapse next to the stems. In some areas of the country there may not be a frost, but one can tell when it is time to dig, because the plants don't look nearly as good as they did in the middle of the season.

Some growers will dig up the clumps prior to the killing frost, as they go south for the winter. This works fine for them, as the tubers have formed nicely during the season and can be successfully stored. One does not necessarily need to get the clumps out of the ground right after the first frost. The only concern is that you would not want the ground to freeze so deep that the eyes of the tubers would freeze. Some growers have been known to toss a thick layer of mulch, leaves, etc. over the garden when they are running late in their digging. This will work fine so long as the eyes do not freeze in the ground below.

If one has two or more of each variety, select the healthiest plant to dig first. If it has sufficient tubers for your needs, then use the tubers from this plant. Try to choose tubers from your healthiest plants and not from those that have not grown well.

Cut the main stalk of the dahlia so that 3-4 inches shows above the ground. Take the name tag that was attached to the stake and attach it to the remaining stump. Using a spade or digging fork, insert the tool to encircle the clump, usually about 12 inches from the stem. Most tubers are within the 7 inches, but you will soon know that there are a few that produce long tubers that will be cut across by the spade (ie. *Kenora Majestic, Akita No Hikari*). With these cultivars, a wider girth can be made. Also, just because a tuber is cut across does not mean that it is destroyed. We will discuss this in the next chapter.

Once the encirclement is finished, leave one spade in the ground and take a second spade and thrust it into the ground at the opposite ends of the clump. By pushing the two handles apart, the clump will rise up carefully. The trick in doing careful digging is to keep the tubers from "breaking their necks". The neck part of the tuber is the most vulnerable, and if the neck is severely broken, the tuber will most likely rot during storage. So, with both hands, lift the clump up and try to remove some of

Broken Neck

the soil attached. Then take a hose and squirt off the remaining soil so that the clump is nice and clean. You will now be able to see the eyes and their relationship to the tubers in the clump. Eyes are not like potatoes. The eyes in tubers will appear close to the stalk.

Dividing the Dahlia Clumps

Most serious dahlia growers will divide the clumps into tubers in the fall. A few will put them away as full clumps and cut them up in the following spring. Storing whole clumps does take up a lot of room.

Dividing tubers is perhaps the most difficult lesson to teach a new dahlia grower. It is much like trying to write out how to ride a bicycle. Watching an experienced dahlia grower cut up the clump and then doing it yourself under supervision is the best way to learn. However, by using pictures and text, an attempt will be made to explain the technique. If possible find a dahlia society since they usually designate a meeting in the fall for demonstrating methods of dividing dahlia clumps.

The wet, dripping clumps can be dealt with immediately, but if this is not possible, put a piece of plastic or wet cloth over it. Don't leave the clumps out in the sun or where it is warm, as they tend to dry out quite rapidly.

When you are ready to cut up the clumps, you will need the tools that are pictured. If you use a small knife, please remember to wear a leather glove on the opposite hand, as very serious cuts can occur. Portions of the clump are very tough and others are very easy to cut through. A pair of short, strong clippers that do not have wide blades is perfect for this job. Deal with only one clump at a time, and take the name tag off of the stalk. Place it next to the clump where the cut up tubers will be placed.

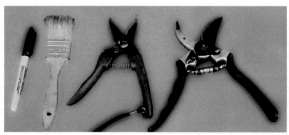

Tools of the trade

Cleaned dahlia clump

Observe where the tuber is attached to the stalk, as there will be a bulging area on the tuber just where it attaches. This is the crown, and this is where the eye or eyes will be found. Simply take the clippers or knife and cut off the crown from the stalk. Trim the tuber of the tiny roots that are projecting from it. Set the trimmed tubers aside on the name tag as they are cut free from the clump.

Tubers cut from stalk

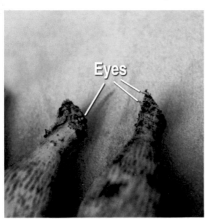

Note crowns with eyes

Many times there will not be a definite eye or shoot. There might be a very slight bulge or even a central depression in the crown. These are probably eyes. If the crown is totally smooth, there is less of a chance that the tuber will have an eye coming forth in the spring. Many growers chose to save most of these tubers, knowing that some will be blind (having no eyes) and, of course, will not grow. The "mother root" is the tuber that was planted last season to produce the dahlia plant itself. This tuber is usually discarded, as it has a good chance of developing fungus over the storage season. The newly developed tubers are a much better choice for storage.

The tubers that lie on the topside of the clump are easy to remove, and many of them have fairly prominent eyes. The lower tubers will be more difficult to cut from the clump and more difficult to locate the eyes. You may encounter situations where there are two tubers attached to a crown, and these may be taken and stored together. They can be further divided in the spring if desired. Proceed to cut the tubers from the clump until there are no more useable tubers. You may try cutting the stem in half, dividing the clump into two halves—or even four quarters. This may allow better visualization of the remaining tubers. Tubers that are smaller than your little finger are usually not worth saving. Tubers that have very slender necks will usually not survive the storage process, as the necks tend to dry out—no matter what you do. Sometimes if the clump has tubers that are slender, cut the clump so that 3 or 4 tubers will be in a group. By putting a strip of masking tape around the bodies of these divisions, the grouping will be more stable and have less chance of breaking individual necks.

A pint jar can be filled with 1 part bleach and 10 parts of water. This is used to sterilize a sharp knife. The tubers that have cuts in them from the digging procedure can now be sliced so that they have nice, smooth, non-contaminated surfaces. These will most likely heal over nicely during storage. The large tubers can be cut across so that 3-4 inches of the tuber and its crown remain. Dealing with an excessively large tuber is cumbersome and rather unnecessary. Also, the cutting tools can be quickly dipped into the bleach water when a new clump is ready to be cut up. This is intended to stop disease transmission from variety to variety.

Some tuber clumps may be configured in such a way that you cannot discern any eyes. This tends to happen with cultivars that have round tubers with little or no necks (ie. *Billy; Rejman's Midnight Pom*). They look like small golf balls that are stuck onto the stem. In this situation just make a parallel cut down the length of the stem and store it as two halves.

Some cultivars are notorious as poor tuber makers (ie. *Camano Cloud, Red Velvet*), and you will be lucky to have one or two decent tubers from the clump. Other cultivars will produce a large number of tubers with eyes that are ideal in size and shape (ie. *Juanita, Jomanda,*

Rebecca Lynn). Whatever the case, if you can get two tubers with eyes from each clump, remember that you will have twice as many plants for your garden next season!

The pile of tubers that you have generated from the clump are now still wet if you have cut them up immediately after digging. In about 6-12 hours, the skins of the tubers will be dry enough to write on. By putting the name of the cultivar or other identifying mark, you will never have any trouble knowing which tuber is which when you want to plant. The writing can be done with a sharp pointed felt marker or with an "indelible pencil" when the tuber is still slightly damp. After labeling the tubers, some growers will not treat the tubers with a fungicide. Others do like to treat the tubers with a fungicide in an attempt to prevent the tubers from rotting over the winter. Powdered sulfur, Cleary's 3336, or Captan have all been used successfully. The sulfur can be lightly dusted on the tubers, especially the cut areas. Sulfur and the other products can be diluted with water according to the manufacturer's directions. The tubers are then submerged into the solution for 15 minutes, removed, and allowed to dry

Those growers who cut their clumps up in the fall will be dealing with a clump that is fairly easy to cut through. If you chose to cut in the spring, the tubers are tougher and drier, making for more difficulty in cutting. If you dig and cut them in the spring, always dust them with sulfur or other fungicide, as they do have a tendency to rot. There is also the problem of shoots appearing in the spring. Any vibration from the cut can cause the shoots to break off from the tuber. If this happens, the base of the shoot that was broken will develop additional shoots from its surface. The only problem is that you will have lost 2 weeks in the growing process.

Storing the Tubers Over the Winter

For those who divide their dahlia tubers in the fall, there are many ways of storing them over the winter. Two popular methods will be presented that seek to accomplish two goals: 1. Protect the tubers from drying out by the time spring rolls around. 2. Prevent the tubers from becoming too wet, causing total destruction by fungus.

The Vermiculite-Plastic Bag Method: The tubers, whether or not they have been dipped into the fungicide solution, will need to dry for about two days. Putting them in a cool place and not on a cement floor will give just the right amount of drying without causing them to shrivel up. You will <u>not</u> want to put them in a warm room with low humidity. Proper drying will cause a protective callus to form over the cuts that were made in the tubers at the time of dividing.

Vermiculite can be purchased from any number of nurseries and garden supply centers. Make sure that the vermiculite is dry, as occasionally there are damp products that do not work well. Several tubers of the same variety are placed in the plastic bag, and vermiculite is poured over them. You will want a little more volume of vermiculite than you have in volume of tubers. Toss the tag into the bag for use next season. Most growers leave the bags open and place them in a paper bag or cardboard box with the topside up. Other growers put in twice as much vermiculite volume as tuber volume and close the bags up tight. Make sure to use a mask when using vermiculite.

The tubers should be checked monthly for rot. Those bad tubers are removed so that the fungus will not infect the remainder of the tubers in the bag.

Plastic Wrap Method: After the tubers are cut from the clump, they can sit for a couple of hours so they are damp, but not dripping wet. They can also be allowed to dry in about 12-24 hours so that you can write the name on each of the tubers with a sharp pointed marker or "Bottle of Ink" pencil. Use a heavy-duty plastic bag and put in one and a half cups of dry vermiculite. To this, add one fourth of a cup of powdered sulfur. Take 3-7 dahlia tubers and put them in the bag, shake for a few seconds, and remove from the bag using a gloved hand. The tubers will be lightly coated with the powdered sulfur. If the tubers are too wet or if the sulfur is excessive in amount, a messy, thick coating will occur. With continued sulfuring of the tubers, you will notice that the coating is a little less than desirable, and that is the time to add a little more powdered sulfur to the bag.

Cut off a piece of plastic wrap about 2 feet long and place it on a table or other flat surface. Beginning at one end of the plastic wrap, place a tuber down and roll the plastic wrap over one complete turn. Lay another along side and roll again. Be certain that no tuber is touching another; plastic wrap must separate all tubers. You may wrap up 5-7 tubers of the same variety in each package, depending on how big the tubers are. In the last 6 inches, fold over the ends and continue to roll until you form a tight package of dahlia tubers. Take a piece of masking tape written with the name of the variety and tape the package shut. The package can be put in a box and filled to the top with packages of tubers. There is no need to provide for air circulation in this method, as the packages are almost airtight.

There is no need to check these packages during the storage period. If a tuber becomes rotted from fungus, it will not infect the other tubers, as the plastic wrap will not allow the fungus to enter the adjacent tuber in the package.

In consideration of the two causes for tuber loss during storage, drying is prevented by having an airtight seal within the package. Some packages will show condensation of water on the inside, but this is of no concern. The second cause for tuber loss is rotting due to fungus. This is prevented by the addition of the sulfur. Within the package a small amount of the powdered sulfur will be converted to sulfur dioxide that is a rather potent fungicide. The airtight package keeps the sulfur dioxide concentrated around the tubers.

The sulfur is usually sold in 4-pound bags for about $5, but some nurseries put it out in the spring and will put it away into storage in the fall (right when you need it). You may have to search around for this product or even purchase it on the Internet.

The plastic wrap method has the disadvantage of taking a little more time and having a little more expense involved. Its advantage is that the space necessary for the storage is much less, and the tubers do not need to be checked during the storage period.

The tubers prepared from either method should be stored in an area that is 35-50 degrees F. If the tubers freeze, their eye will be lost and the tuber will turn to mush. If the temperature is too high, the tubers will sprout. New growers commonly make the mistake of thinking that their basement is plenty cool, but most basements are much warmer than the desired temperature. Disaster strikes when the grower looks at the tubers in the middle of January, and 4 inch sprouts are coming out of their tubers! Putting a thermometer on the boxes of tubers can be helpful in determining the proper storage temperature. A few thoughts might be a crawl space or a neighbor who goes to Florida in the winter (and keeps the home at 45 degrees). It is more difficult for those in warmer climates to find a cold enough environment to store the dahlia tubers.

Chapter Twelve

Taking Cuttings from Dahlias

by Richard W. Peters, M.D.

When the shoots have emerged from the eyes of the dahlia tubers, cuttings can be made using this fairly easy process. The advantages to taking cuttings are three-fold. First, you can propagate extra plants from a single tuber, which is great if the tuber is an expensive one. Second, since gardening is a hobby, you can begin working with your plants a month earlier than usual. This extends the pleasure of your hobby. Third, cuttings give extra plants of a variety which serve as back-up plants in case the tuber rots and does not produce the mother plant. The cuttings will then be available to grow and take the place of the rotted plant, or you will have the joy of sharing extra plants with your friends.

Counting back about ten weeks from when you think you would ordinarily plant your dahlias into the garden, the tuber desired for cuttings is taken out of storage. Place it in a container filled with moist, but not wet, potting soil. Make sure the crown of the tuber is right at the top level of the potting soil. Place a cover over the container in order to prevent moisture loss. Place the planting in a warm area, such as the top of a refrigerator, so that the tuber will begin to form roots and produce shoots. By observing the planted tuber every few days, you will see the shoot begin to emerge from the soil. At this time remove the covering, and place the container under fluorescent lights. Use an 18-hour light—6-hour darkness cycle; the lights will stimulate the plant to grow.

You will need a supply of 4 oz Styrofoam fruit cups and 12 oz hard, clear plastic cups. You can purchase these containers from a kitchen supply or party store. Often organizations use the clear plastic cups when serving a beverage at a meeting, and this is a good place to salvage cups for your cuttings. Make sure that the plastic cup will fit over the top of the Styrofoam cup, as you will want a nice, firm fit. It is a lot of trouble if the plastic cup's diameter is the same size as the Styrofoam cup. Put 4-6 holes in the lowest part of the side of the 4 oz cup for drainage. Label the cup with the name of the cultivar and the date. Fill the cup almost to the top with high quality, sterile potting soil. With a dibble (sharp, pointed stick), put a central hole in the soil where the cutting will be placed.

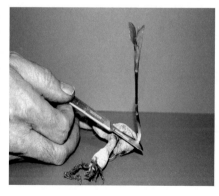

When the shoot is about 3 inches tall and has one or two pairs of good leaves, it is ready for cutting. Carefully lift up the crown of the tuber and observe the area where the shoot is emerging from the crown. Using a razor blade, #10 scalpel blade, or a thin knife, cut the shoot about 1/16 of an inch above the tuber's crown. You will find a pair of rudimentary leaves in this area, and the cut is usually made right in the lower part of the stem from where these leaves emerge. Trim off these rudimentary leaves.

Where to make the cut

The cut base of the dahlia shoot is then dipped into a rooting hormone that also contains a fungicide. Do not allow the hormone powder to cake onto the cutting, and tap the cutting onto the surface of the bench top to remove excess. Insert the cutting into the hole in the potting soil and firm the soil around it. Carefully pour water into the 4 oz cup so that the soil is completely wet. Push on the top of the soil so that extra water comes out of the drainage holes. Then place the plastic cup over the Styrofoam cup in a secure fashion. The cutting is then placed under fluorescent lights so that the light is just above the top of the 12 oz plastic cup. You will not have to water the cutting, as it is a self-contained terrarium.

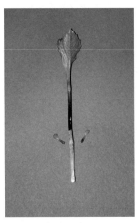  

Trim low leaves and dip base into rooting hormone   *Insert cutting into potting soil*   *Water and cover, creating a terrarium.*

Steps in taking dahlia cittings

Within the cup, the cutting produces food from its leaves exposed to the light. Roots usually begin to form in 16-20 days, and the plant will begin to grow. At this time, the top cup can be removed, and the cup with the cutting can be inverted, holding on to the soil with your hand. Along the edges of the soil, roots can be seen if the cutting is well rooted. If no roots are seen, replace the clear plastic cup and store under the light for a few more days. If roots are present, then pot up the cutting, trying not to disturb the soil of the cutting.

At this time, the young rooted cutting is vulnerable to a striking change in humidity. It has spent its life so far in 100% humidity and now will be thrust into low humidity of the home. Simply dry the plastic 12 oz cup and place it at an angle over the cutting in its new pot. Place the cup in such a way as to allow a little air circulation by balancing the plastic cup on the topside of the pot. By allowing this minimal air circulation, you will aid the cutting in adjusting to lower humidity over the next 2-3 days. Then completely remove the plastic cup. You can either place the plant in sunshine or place it back under the lights. If you do not go through this procedure to deal with humidity change, you will cause the plant to lose the vitality of its leaves, and the plant may be lost.

In a few days after you have taken your first cutting from the tuber, the cut surface of the crown will heal over and begin to form 2-3 more shoots. When these get up to about 3 inches with one or two good pair of leaves, you can then make additional cuttings by following the same procedure. The area will again heal over and begin to form additional shoots. Some growers indicate that 12-14 cuttings have been obtained from a single tuber, but usually more like 6 should be the norm. At some point you may actually tire of taking cuttings from the same variety!

Once you have a plant in its pot, it is treated just like a plant that is springing from a tuber. When successful, the new grower will have a real sense of accomplishment in having propagated a desired dahlia.

Chapter Thirteen

Why Didn't My Dahlias Grow Well this Season?

by Richard W. Peters, M.D.

This question is not uncommon among those of us who are beginning to try our hand at raising these flowers. It is a bit discouraging, I am sure, but if you know some of the reasons that dahlias do not grow well, you can become more successful next season. Let's go over some of the reasons that a dahlia may not grow well:

Sun Problems

1. If a dahlia does not have access to at least 5 hours of sun, it usually is not able to generate enough food supply through photosynthesis to produce blooms. The growth may be stunted or gangly. If you suspect that inadequate amounts of sun may be your problem, consider doing an analysis for sun-hours in your plot. With a pencil and paper, check the plot every two hours throughout the day. Begin at 8 am and go until

Withought at least 5 hours of sun, the dahlia is not able to generate enough food supply through photosynthesis.

there is no more sun shining on the plot. Then you will know for sure if this is a proper place to plant the dahlias. If you can prune away limbs from trees that are blocking out the sun, then you may be able to increase the sun hours allowing you to raise dahlias in that area.

2.   If a dahlia is planted very close to a white house or building, there may be excessive heat generated that would inhibit the plant from growing properly. Also, trying to grow dahlias in heat zones of 7-12 will usually end up being unsuccessful unless extraordinary means are utilized.

Water Problems

1.   The type of soil the plant is growing in and the amount of natural rainfall will both determine the amount of additional water that will be needed. Dahlias planted in sand on hot days will need watering every other day. This is because sandy soil allows water to pass through it with little retention. Dahlias planted in heavy, clay soil with cool days may not need any watering until conditions change. Dahlias hate over watering and puddles, and in these conditions their roots and tubers may begin to rot.

2.   Insufficient watering of dahlias will also stunt its growth. The leaves will be small and tend to turn brown. The plants can wilt in the late morning to early evening. Generally, the plant will not produce blooms or they will be quite small.

Nutrient Problems

1.   Improper soil conditions can hamper the growth of a dahlia plant. By taking soil samples in the late fall, you will know what needs to be added to the soil to create an atmosphere that is ideal for dahlia plants. A pH that is too high or too low will inhibit the plant from taking up necessary elements and molecules needed for its growth.

Good soil preparation prior to planting a dahlia is extremely important. Mixing in compost, humus, and other vegetable matter will allow good aeration of your soil. The roots of the dahlia will thrive under these conditions. Gardeners use composted manures, grass clippings, leaves, straw, mushroom compost, and vegetable matter with good success. Pay attention to the source and quality of the compost that you are adding to your garden. You would not want a contaminant of heavy metal, fir bark mulch with turpentine, or long-acting weed killer to be present.

2.   If the dahlia plant is put in the ground where roots from adjacent trees or shrubs are present, their roots may envelope the roots of the dahlia. The dahlia will have difficulty getting adequate moisture and nutrients from the soil, as the other roots will rob the dahlia. This results in a stunted dahlia plant. One solution to this problem is use a gallon container with holes in it to pot up your dahlia tuber. Then bury the entire pot in the ground being careful to water and fertilize the entire area and not just the pot. Otherwise, the undesired roots from outside the pot will travel through the holes in the pot to get at the better supply of water and fertilizer inside the pot.

The dahlia will have difficulty getting sun and adequate moisture and nutrients here, as the other roots will rob the dahlia.

Diseased Plant Problems

1.   Aphids can be a real problem with dahlias. Check plants often so that early detection and proper treatment are undertaken before the pests do a lot of damage. Aphids get into the tips of the growing areas of the plant and begin to multiply by bearing their young alive. They suck the juices from the tender tips and cause the leaves to curl and the plant to cease growing properly. One can direct a spray of water onto the areas of infestation and dislodge these insects. If this fails, an insecticidal soap or an insecticide that will handle aphids can be used.

2.   Spider mites are a real threat to the dahlia plant. They begin in hot weather by infecting the undersides of the lower leaves. These leaves turn brown and may have a slight web produced on the under leaf. You need to act fairly quickly, as mites will travel up the plant and kill it. To make the diagnosis, take off one or two of the infected leaves and bang it over a piece of white paper on a table. Then take a magnifying glass and watch for small dots that begin to move over the surface of the paper. The mites can be handled by spraying water upwards onto the bottom surfaces of the leaves. This dislodges the mites, and they are believed to die when this happens. Insecticidal soap, Avid, Kelthane, and Malathion can be used as miticides. Just be sure to treat the undersurface of the leaves.

3.   Powdery mildew is a fungal disease that regularly affects dahlias. The dahlia can be infected with mildew anytime that growth appears above the ground. Giving adequate spacing between plants to promote air circulation is a wonderful way to prevent this disease. Powdery mildew will cause a plant to grow poorly and loose its leaves. Severe infections will also destroy the blooms and buds.

One must prevent the disease from spreading. By spraying with a fungicide that handles powdery mildew, you will protect the upper, newly forming leaves from becoming infected, but you will not return the diseased leaves to normal. You will see a resurgence of the dahlia plants in just a few days. Propiconazole, sulfur, and copper sulfate have been used with success.

4.   When the dahlia plant is first planted in the early spring, there is danger from slugs and snails. These pests will eat the first tender tips of your plant so that it will be stunted and not grow well at all. Watch for them early in the morning when the dew is still on the plants. An iron phosphorus type of snail bait works best. It is not toxic to you or the environment, but it sure does take care of these critters. Continue checking for these unwelcome pests throughout the growing season.